The Golden Years
1903-1913

1   The very essence of Edwardian security and serenity has been captured here. A. E. Housman's verse epitomises such trees and such young people:

Loveliest of trees, the cherry now
Is hung with bloom along the bough,
And stands about the woodland ride
Wearing white for Eastertide.

Now, of my threescore years and ten,
Twenty will not come again,
And take from seventy springs a score,
It only leaves me fifty more.

And since to look at things in bloom
Fifty springs are little room,
About the woodlands I will go
To see the cherry hung with snow.

The Golden Years
1903-1913

*A pictorial survey of the most interesting
decade in English history, recorded in
contemporary photographs and drawings*

GORDON WINTER

DAVID & CHARLES : NEWTON ABBOT LONDON

Οὐ Κλειοι ἀλλα Θαλεια

0 7153 6896 6

Set in 11 on 13 pt Times Roman
Photoset and printed in Great Britain
by REDWOOD BURN LIMITED, Trowbridge and Esher
for David & Charles (Holdings) Limited
South Devon House Newton Abbot Devon

Contents

Acknowledgements

I gratefully acknowledge the following sources of photographs and drawings in this book, and express my appreciation of the kindness and patience shown me by all the individuals concerned. Plate 1, Victoria & Albert Museum (Agnes B. Warburg Collection). Plates 2, 13, 14, 40, 41, 128, John and Susan Wareham. 3, 15a, b, c, 38, 55, 107, 114, 115, 120, 126, 134, *Country Life*. 4, 7, 8, 9, Dr Stephen Coffin. 5, 10, 11, 31, 34, 42, 51, 52, 53, 69, 70, 73, 75, 76, 77, 78, 79, 80, 82, 95, 103, 124, 131, Kodak Museum. 6, 48, 50, 91, 108, 127, Suffolk Photographic Survey. 12, 16, 18, 20, 21, 28, 29, 30, 33, 39, 49, 57, 58, 59, 60, 61, 81, 85, 87, 88, 89, 93, 94, 102, 109, 135, 136, 137, 138, 139, *Punch*. 17, 23, National Trust. 19, 24, 25, 26, 27, 32, 36, 37, 47, 56, 90, 130, 132, *Illustrated London News*. 22, *Everybody's Weekly*. 35, 86, 121, 129, J. Barton. 44, 45, 54, *Cassell's Household Guide*. 43, 71, 83, 84, 99, *Boy's Own Paper*. 46, 72, 96, 97, Major and Mrs George Cree. 62, 63, 64, 65, 66, Oxfordshire County Education Officer. 67, Tower Hamlets Public Library. 68, Greater London Council. 74, 98, 104, 105, 106, 117, 118, 119, 122, East Sussex Museum Service. 92, Exeter Public Library. 100, 101, 123, 125, Dorchester Public Library. 110, 111, 112, D. G. Valentine. 113, 116, A. J. Huxley. 133, Mrs H. G. D. Stuart. 140, 141, 142, Court of Assistants, Honourable Artillery Company.

I am also grateful to the following for permission to reproduce poems, and for quotations in the text: from Philip Larkin's *The Whitsun Weddings*, (Faber and Faber Ltd); from A. E. Housman's 'The Shropshire Lad', (The Society of Authors as the literary representative of the Estate of A. E. Housman; and Jonathan Cape Ltd, publishers of A. E. Housman's *Collected Poems*); from Donald Read's *Edwardian England*, (George G. Harrap); from Flora Thompson's *Lark Rise to Candleford*, (Oxford University Press); and from Gabriel Tschumi's *Royal Chef*, (William Kimber).

Foreword

The ten years between 1903 and 1913 were the most interesting ten years in English history. Whether they were in fact the Golden Years, as the title of this book implies, is debatable. It is only too easy to point to the social injustices of the period, and to the mistakes that were made; even so, taken all round, the years were probably as good for the great majority of the population as any ten years before or since. What characterised them above all else is that they were years of golden promise. England still maintained the wealth, the power, the self-confidence and the sense of purpose that had marked the Victorian era. At the same time the worst of the evils of the nineteenth century were at last being brought to an end. Between 1903 and 1913 there reached the Statute Book the beginnings of the most important social legislation that this country had yet known.

State old-age pensions were first paid out from post offices throughout the country in 1909. The National Insurance Act of 1911 provided for the first time a system of national insurance against unemployment, though it was limited to certain trades liable to cyclical fluctuations, and in January 1913 began the first national contributory sickness insurance. On these foundations was built the whole of our modern edifice of the Welfare State. Public education leaped forward at an equal pace. In the ten years between 1903 and 1913 the money spent by local authorities on education in England and Wales increased from under £10 million to over £30 million; Whitehall expenditure on education nearly doubled. The same ten years saw the birth or rebirth of the universities of Liverpool and Manchester in 1903, Leeds in 1904, Sheffield in 1905 and the Imperial College of Science in 1907; the significance of the emphasis on science and technology at all these universities, which was to rescue British higher education from the classical doldrums, was perhaps hardly realised at the time.

Above all else, every man, woman and child in the country believed without question in the splendid inevitability of progress. Things were better than they had been in grandfather's day; and they would continue to get better, slowly and almost effortlessly, as the years went by.

It is of course obvious that the same ten years saw the growth of the destructive forces that led to the first World War. Only on a very superficial analysis can one claim that by beginning at 1903 and ending at 1913 we avoid the Boer War at one end and the first rumblings of the World War at the other. Of the Boer War it is true; of the World War it is not true at all. If we accept Von Clausewitz's dictum that war is only diplomacy carried on by other means, then the first World War began in the nineteenth century, perhaps as early as 1870. By the opening years of the twentieth century many informed people must have believed, though they seldom admitted it, that war between England and Germany was inevitable. Sometimes they even got the date right. Notice Mr Punch's astonishingly accurate shot on page 109. None of that, however, diminished the golden light—golden sunset perhaps—that shone on the brief period in English history with which this book is concerned. The sun had not yet gone down. It had hardly even dipped behind the trees.

We continue to look back on the years before 1914 as the last years of English normality; the years before everything that seemed enduring began to break up and change. But the idea that all the great social improvements that we have seen in our time, including the establishment of the Welfare State, were the result of the two World Wars (one following so closely on the heels of the other as to make them virtually one war) is, I believe, largely untrue. The changes for the better, the social improvements, were already on their way before 1914. And they were being brought in more smoothly and painlessly, with less destruction of the good traditions of the past, essentially because they were taking place without the wastage of war. It is interesting to ponder what English life would have been like by 1975 if we had been able to settle our differences with Germany without bloodshed.

What I have attempted to do in this brief and casual study is to reflect something of the glow that suffused the landscape in the Golden Years. For those who were lucky enough to live in them they offered a sense of well-being and security that has never been known since. The question: 'What would life be like now if progress had gone on without a break in 1914?' is worth considering because, if we knew the answer, we should be able to understand more clearly where we have gone wrong.

Readers of my two previous picture books, *A Country Camera* and *Past Positive* (A Cockney Camera), may wonder why this volume is not confined to photographs but includes drawings from magazines as well. It seems to me that there is a particular advantage in this combination. A photograph taken in 1903 is likely to show us what people actually looked like at that time. Magazines of the period, however, were not mainly illustrated with photographs; they were lavishly illustrated with drawings and engravings, many of which were based on photographs but deliberately 'improved', at least in terms of what the artist considered to be an improvement. Magazine drawings tended to show people not as they were but as they liked to think they were. By comparing the drawings and the photographs we can probably get a more accurate impression of the aspirations and achievements of ordinary men and women of the period than we could from photographs alone. For convenience, I have used the term Edwardian throughout these pages to include the first four years of the reign of George V.

No book of this kind could have been compiled without much help from many people. I am indebted to Mr Peter Castle and Miss Caroline Odgers of the Victoria & Albert Museum, Mr Brian Coe of the Kodak Museum, Miss Stephanie Glover of the Royal United Service Institution and Miss Stella Hardy of Tonbridge Public Library for assistance and advice. Dr Stephen Coffin, Major and Mrs George Cree, Dr and Mrs Thomas Hills, Mr Anthony Huxley, Lieutenant-Colonel Paddy Massey, Mrs Dennis Shand, Mrs H. G. D. Stuart and Mr and Mrs John Wareham have generously lent me books and photographs from private collections. In culling material from magazines of the period I have been particularly indebted to the editors of *Country Life*, of *Punch* and of the *Illustrated London News*. Mr Reg Thompson has devoted unstinted time and skill to the copying of photographs and drawings, many of which have been deftly retouched by Mr David Ryder. In particular I would like to thank Mr Philip Larkin and his publishers, Faber & Faber, for allowing me to include his poem *MCMXIV* from *The Whitsun Weddings*. So far as facts and figures are concerned, much the most convenient source of historical information about the period is Professor Donald Read's *Edwardian England* (Harrap, 1972), on which I have shamelessly drawn. Those who want to dig deeper than I have attempted to do in these casual pages should turn to Professor Read's book, and to his *Documents from Edwardian England*.

The age of innocence

2   In the days before hens lived in batteries: In the early days of the century, almost every family that had a plot of land at the back of the house kept their own chickens. Feeding the hens and collecting the eggs was every child's privilege and pleasure. This little girl seems to have fed them from the bowl in which she has measured out the grain; from my own early recollections, she would have been just as likely to have carried the grain in her pinafore. Keeping chickens was not confined to those who lived in the country or on the edge of a town. Poultry were commonplace in suburban gardens. The contented clucking of a dozen hens provided an agreeable background to the sounds of daily life, though light sleepers in the suburbs were liable to complain about the crowing of cocks.

3 A sense of continuity: When this photograph was taken, nearly a hundred years had passed since England had last been engaged in a life-and-death struggle. Perhaps for that reason, there was a sense of permanence about Edwardian family life that is hardly known today. The picture, by the Victorian photographer Henry Peach Robinson, was published in *Country Life* in December 1903 shortly after his death, under the title *Dawn and Sunset*. Robinson was known for his composite photographs, designed to look as much like paintings as possible, and this one is true to form. It would not, however, have struck readers as particularly nostalgic or dated in 1903. The furniture, the clothes and the characters could have been found in most English villages at the time. The importance of the soap and water in Robinson's composition is probably not accidental; cleanliness was central to the Edwardian concept of life. The idea that because cottages did not have bathrooms the inhabitants did not keep themselves clean is absurdly wrong; they enjoyed the pleasure of bathing by the fireside, and by firelight, which we have forgotten.

Domesticity

That the quality of domestic life depends on those who take part in it, rather than on their surroundings, is a truth that needs little arguing. However, the surroundings help. It is easy to be unhappy in a mansion; it is even easier to be unhappy in a hovel. In looking at the quality of life in a past decade, the housing is therefore a good place to begin. In the following section I have tried to show something of what Edwardian housing was like at the beginning of the era, of the great strides that were made in improving it, and what it might have been like had the progress been allowed to continue without a break.

The Edwardians turned with horror from the industrial housing that they had inherited from the previous century. But they did not turn, as they might easily have done, to a *Bauhaus* dream of steel and concrete and glass. From urban squalor they looked back to the lost paradise, or supposed paradise, of a country cottage set in green fields under a blue sky. From this dream there sprang the garden city and the garden suburb. Places like Letchworth and Hampstead Garden Suburb remind us of how effective the Edwardian dreamers could be when they woke up.

4   The kind of housing that the Edwardians wanted to get rid of: Because terraces of this kind have acquired the patina of age, we today no longer regard them as necessarily ugly or evil in themselves. What made them evil seventy years ago was usually the industrial background against which they were built. Not a few such terraces, if they now have a convenient address, have been upgraded and turned into sought-after middle-class homes. Even at the beginning of this century they probably provided a better chance of a cohesive local community than do the monstrous blocks of local-authority flats that have been built in the past twenty-five years. At least the drab terraces were on a human scale. Nevertheless, this particular photograph appeared, in an album in 1903, as an example of the kind of housing to be avoided.

5 Rural dream and rural reality: This child, photographed in about 1904, is wearing what may have been her grandmother's bonnet, and she was obviously posed by a photographer in search of the picturesque. But the interior of the cottage is genuine enough. It offered the simple comforts of rural life as they had continued, little changed, for many centuries. The kettle hanging over the fire provided constant hot water on a small scale. If you wanted hot water on a more lavish scale you lit the copper, on the right. For many cottagers, firewood was to be had for the labour of gathering it. This was a cherished privilege, because it had such an important influence on the cottager's cost of living.

6   Water from the well: An Edwardian country housewife thought herself lucky, as did her mother and grandmother, in having her own well in the garden. Anyone, however, who has known the labour of winding up every bucket of water that is wanted in the house (as we did at one time during my own childhood) will never take tap water for granted. A well in the garden had its problems. Unless there was plenty of space, it was difficult to avoid putting the privy—usually at the end of the garden—closer to the well than it should have been.

7   Asmuns Place, Hampstead Garden Suburb: A photograph that was used by the founders of Hampstead Garden Suburb as a contrast to the terrace housing in plate 4. It shows precisely what the Garden Suburb was trying to do and what it so successfully achieved. The proposal to form a Garden Suburb at Hampstead was put before the readers of *The Times* on 13 January, 1906. The contributor explained that the project was possible because, adjoining Hampstead Heath, there was an estate of 320 acres which had belonged to Eton College since the time of Henry VI. At the instance of Mrs S. A. Barnett (Henrietta Barnett) of Toynbee Hall, Whitechapel, the college were offering this estate to the public. Eighty acres was to be added to Hampstead Heath and the remainder laid out as a garden suburb.

The article commented: 'The practicability of such an extension of London once proved, the character of suburb-making may be expected to undergo a change. It will be realised that an estate on the outskirts of a great town may, at a reasonable profit, be so developed as to provide a pleasant residence not only for the rich, but for all classes. Public opinion may well demand that town extension shall follow on some such lines.'

8 & 9   Waterlow Court, Hampstead Garden Suburb: Waterlow Court was designed as a women's hostel, or rather as a ladies' hostel in the terminology of its day. These photographs of a top-floor and a first-floor suite provide a wonderful record of Edwardian interior decoration and of the high standard that the flats offered. The photographs have survived because they were preserved in an album presented to Mrs Barnett on 16 November, 1912, and signed by all the 47 original residents of Waterlow Court, which was specifically designed for single working women.

The Hampstead Garden Suburb is recognised as part of England's architectural heritage and is as important in its way as, say, Broadway in Worcestershire. Unfortunately, its houses and flats are now far beyond the means of the kind of people for whom they were originally intended.

10   Home entertainment before television: Few informal interior shots of Edwardian homes have come down to us. This one, by an unknown photographer in 1903, is preserved by the Kodak Museum either because it was taken by a member of the Kodak staff or, more probably, because it was submitted in a competition for amateur snapshots.

11   At the nursery door: Another informal Edwardian interior, taken in about 1904 by evening light without a flash. Lack of money prevented many such Edwardian middle-class homes from falling into the error of over-decoration and over-furnishing that spoiled the wealthier houses of the period.

12   An upper middle-class drawing room of 1903: I have taken this picture from *Punch*, in spite of the feeble joke, because it provides such an unselfconscious record of clothes and furniture. The kettle with the spirit lamp under it was an essential part of the English Tea Ceremony, and survived into my own childhood. The lamp in the background is oil-burning, though it might just have been electric.

FOR THE COMING ACADEMY.

Young Mrs. Jim (the visitor). "So sorry I'm late, dear, but Jim has been making me sit to Mr. Pallitt, and I've been there all the afternoon."
Mrs. Elderson (at home). "Oh, is Pallitt painting you? Then all I can say is, I only hope he will flatter you more than he did me!"

13 & 14   Happiness is a garden and a greenhouse: We do not know the names or indeed anything about the characters in the two photographs, taken inside and outside the same greenhouse, but their sense of well-being is evident. The gentleman with the watch-chain is a good example of the theory that men and women develop faces to conform with the age in which they live. Compare this man with H. G. Wells and many others of his period.

20 OR 250 ACRES WITH RESIDENCE.

WARWICKSHIRE AND GLOUCES-
TERSHIRE.—
Moreton-in-the-Marsh district.—For SALE at "Times"
price, an attractive RESIDENTIAL ESTATE of 250
acres. The commodious Residence is well retired from
the road, and has
ESTABLISHED GROUNDS AND FINE TIMBER.
Apply TRESIDDER & CO., 21, Cockspur St., S.W. (5590.)

GOLF, BOATING, FISHING, HUNTING.

PRICE ONLY £2,000

HERTS (1½ miles main line station).—Charming
COTTAGE RESIDENCE with, two
acres: four reception, eight bedrooms; stabling; partly
walled kitchen garden.
Agents, TRESIDDER & CO., 21, Cockspur Street. S.W. (4356.)

£1,750 ONLY.—ESSEX AND SUFFOLK
BORDERS (mile from station and country
town, with R.C. and other churches, etc.).—Above attractive
RESIDENCE, in splendid order, situate in high, healthy
position, with lovely views. Contains pretty drawing room
20ft. by 17ft., dining, morning rooms, five excellent bedrooms
(more could be added), bathroom (h. and c.), etc.; beautifully
laid-out well-timbered secluded grounds, lawns, gardens,
meadowland of FOUR ACRES; stabling, outbuildings,
vinery, etc.; good water; modern sanitation; mile from
river and golf. Early Sale desired.—COBBE & WINCER,
Ipswich.

400ft. above sea level.

Extensive views to the south.   Gravel soil.

£3,750 (WITHIN 25 MILES NORTH OF TOWN).—Well-built Freehold
modern RESIDENCE, in a quiet and secluded situation, in
well-matured gardens of nearly four acres. Entrance hall, dining room with very
large bay, drawing room, library, large conservatory, eight bedrooms, fitted bathrooms. Co.'s water. Main drainage. The House throughout is exceptionally
well fitted with carved mantels and fireplaces. Great care has been expended in
arranging the gardens, which include croquet lawn, terrace, shrubberies, rose
pergolas, well-stocked kitchen garden of about an acre, small orchard, etc. Range
of greenhouses with good bearing vines. Stabling for three, double coach or motor
house. Hunting and golf near.

(Might possibly be Let on Lease.)

Inspected and recommended by HAMPTON & SONS, 2 and 3, Cockspur Street, S.W.

15   At the upper end of the country-house market: Samples from the advertisement pages of *Country Life* of 23 May, 1912, which show how much you could get for your money before inflation robbed us of our currency. Nowadays, when such houses appear on the market, they are almost always for sale free-hold. The Edwardians were more given to letting houses for a few years, or just for the summer.

16   Walking in the park: The habit of country-house visiting, which we are inclined to think of as a development of the 1970s, has in fact been part of the English way of life for many centuries. The celebrated couplet

> *On painted ceilings you devoutly stare*
> *Where sprawl the saints of Verrio and Laguerre*

was written by Pope in 1731. All that has happened since is that the spread of motoring has extended the habit to a wider range of people than was possible when great houses were visited on horseback or in carriages. The problem of politely controlling visitors in the park (invited ones, not poachers) is often as old as the houses. This drawing is from *Punch* of 1905.

'Arry. "HI, THERE! YOU THERE! HI! COME OFF THE GRASS, CAN'T YOU? DON'T YOU SEE THE NOTICE? IT'S THE LIKES OF YOU TRESPASSIN' CHAPS AS MAKES 'EM SHUT THEIR PARKS."
Noble Owner. "OH, I BEG PARDON. I FORGOT THE NOTICE. I'LL COME OFF AT ONCE!"

17   The lap of luxury: The tasteless opulence with which some rich Edwardians were in the habit of furnishing their houses is so familiar that the point is hardly worth making. This picture perhaps states the case more pointedly. It would look lavish if it was a room in a private house; it is in fact in a yacht. The furniture looks Victorian. The leather-bound *Lioyd's Register* on the table is dated 1898, but the binding is so worn that I would guess that the photograph was taken about 1903.

Social contrasts

Edwardian society inherited a situation in which the span between the richest and the poorest was as wide as that of the previous century. The Edwardians differed from the Victorians, however, in that they generally recognised that the span was too great, and that private charity and individual good intentions were not enough to bridge it. In an industrial society the State would have to play a major part. The photographs and drawings in this section are a reminder of how their problems appeared to the Edwardians themselves.

Striker. "THA KNOWS, BILL, IF WE DUNNA MIND, T' MASTERS WILL BE T' BOSSES!"

18   Summing it all up: George Belcher's drawing in *Punch* of 16 November, 1910, epitomises the folly of the struggle between management and labour that has disrupted British industry throughout the twentieth century. In 1910 *Punch* was even more a middle- and upper-class weekly than it is now, so presumably it was the employers rather than potential strikers who were supposed to be amused by the joke. Yet in a curious way it is a joke within a joke. One is left with the feeling that Belcher's sympathies lie with the characters in his drawing and that he is really laughing at those who think that the joke is funny.

19   Hard work as *The Illustrated London News* saw it: This drawing was published in the *ILN* of 10 August, 1907 under the title 'An Apostle of Labour in a Scene of Fierce Toil; Mr Keir Hardie in the Stoke-hold'. Keir Hardie, the second figure from the left, is watching stokers in the Canadian Pacific liner *Empress of Britain*. The editorial comment remarks: 'Mr Keir Hardie was among the passengers who sailed for Canada on July 12 on board the *Empress of Britain*. During the voyage Mr Keir Hardie went down to the stoke-hold and watched the fiercest and most exacting labour to which mortal can be set. The Labour leader was recognised by many of the men. The furnaces of the *Empress of Britain* consume 300 tons of coal a day.' Once again the significance is not what was said but where it was published. The *ILN* was essentially a weekly for upper-middle-class clubs and middle-class homes. The drawing, and the comments on it, are plainly sympathetic to the stokers.

20 & 21 (opposite)   The other side of the coin: *Punch* was not always sympathetic to those who were down on their luck, but both these drawings explain why social problems were not as acute in the

A SAD CASE.

Squire "HAVEN'T HAD A JOB SINCE EASTER, HAVEN'T YOU? WHAT ARE YOU?"
Tramp "I'M AN 'OT CROSS BUN MAKER!"

countryside as they were in the towns. The squire of 1908 who rode the narrow lanes in the saddle never lost touch with the tramp in the hedgerow; if he had driven by in a closed car, the tramp would have been a scarcely noticed figure, separated from him by the glass of the car window.

Similarly, the condescension of the Lady Bountiful of 1903 may have been infuriating to those at the receiving end of her charity, but at least she knew what went on in the village. Even when she drove down the street in her carriage, the carriage was likely to be open so that she would not feel cut off.

22   A new suit for thirty-five shillings, or £1.75: The advertisement in *Everybody's Weekly* of 13 May, 1911 uses the phrase 'This gentlemanly, good wearing suit . . .' to emphasise that enduring characteristic of English society—the aping of those a rung or two above oneself. £1.75 did not seem particularly cheap to the readers of *Everybody's* at the time. The magazine had just been running a series of articles, *Who Are the Middle Classes?* That of 18 March, 1911, entitled 'The Pinch of Poverty on £200 a Year' examines the finances of the Penningtons, who live at Stamford Hill in a six-roomed house. Their £200 a year is described as 'An income that would be luxury to the workman and beggary to the stockbroker . . . Only an infinity of petty economies can save such a household from the quicksands of debt.' The detailed budget went as follows:

DELIVERED
to all approved
orders for 5/-
with Order.
Balance payable
by Six Monthly
Payments of 5/-

35/-

	£	s	d
Rent, rates and taxes	48	17	0
Pennington, personal	41	5	0
Mrs Pennington, clothes and boots	75	12	0
Mrs Pennington, housekeeping			
for self and children	10	0	0
Children's school fees	18	0	0

THE GRAVES 'LUDGATE' SUIT

is, absolutely the last word in popular-priced Tailoring Perfection. This Gentlemanly good-wearing Suit is distinguished by all the points which denote successful and satisfac-

houses, cost the same amount. The great sacrifice, which more than any other marked the family out as middle-class, was the expenditure on school fees.

A few weeks later *Everybody's* examined the budget of a doctor in general practice who allowed £185 a year for his children's education, kept two servants, and lived in considerable comfort on £600 a year. Holidays amounted to 'a week or ten days with his wife on the Continent in the spring, and three weeks or a month in Devon or Cornwall in the summer with the family'. On £600 a year.

Old Woman (to young Lady Bountiful). "YES, MISS, NELLIE DO GROW. SHE SKIPS OUT OF 'ER SHOES IN NO TIME. 'ER FEET ARE TREMENJEOUS. I SHOULD THINK A PAIR OF YOURS WOULD JUST FIT 'ER, MISS!"

23 Big-game hunting in Surrey: In Edwardian England the rich were really rich. Yet somehow or other life at the top of the bracket, especially among those who had recently acquired their wealth, seems to have become unutterably boring. The social columns of the papers of the day described the same people going through the same social ritual year after year simply because it was thought to be the right thing to do. To be a successful hostess you had to persuade the most important people in the land to accept your invitations. The ultimate trophy in big-game hunting of this kind was of course King Edward VII himself. Mrs Ronald Greville, the wife of Captain the Hon Ronald Greville and step-daughter of William McEwan, an immensely wealthy Scottish businessman, is seen in this photograph having achieved the ambition of all hostesses. She is sitting on the King's right hand. She entertained the King on a number of occasions at the Priory, Reigate and at Polesden Lacey, Dorking, houses she and her husband rented but did not own.

If over-eating is a sign of boredom, and almost invariably it is, this part of Edwardian society excelled at it. It was commonplace for an ordinary dinner—not a banquet—at a house like Reigate Priory to consist of eight or nine courses. These were not alternatives, but set in front of the guests one after the other so that it was difficult to avoid eating something of each of them. A typical menu began with caviar, followed by soup, then salmon, then chicken, then lamb cutlets, then a roast, then asparagus, then peaches.

Gabriel Tschumi has given an impressive account of Edwardian gluttony in *Royal Chef*. More telling than his accounts of the vast dinners is a simple picnic lunch for a shooting party: mulligatawny soup, ragout, roast chicken, roast pheasant, apple dumplings, compote of pears, biscuits and pastries. Mr Tschumi adds: 'Dinner that night was usually elaborate to make up for the plain food.'

26

24　Tea on the lawn outside the clubhouse at Ranelagh in July 1907: The artist of this drawing from the *Illustrated London News* has made his characters look less bored than those in the preceding photograph, and they probably were less bored. The caption to the picture claimed that visitors had a choice of polo, gymkhanas, children's plays and good music, and that skilled waiters were 'pledged to serve 1,000 teas in 60 minutes'. At Ranelagh there was usually a chance of meeting someone new and exciting, outside the inevitable round.

25   Big-game hunting in India: A drawing published in the *Illustrated London News* of 1907 as 'the Jam Saheb of Nawanagar's wonderful portable shooting-box in the jungle'. The caption explains that the box is mounted on wheels and can be drawn to a suitable position in the jungle by oxen or elephants, and left until the animals grow accustomed to it. 'The Jam Saheb will then take up his abode' explained the caption, 'and will be ready for his quarry at any time of day or night . . . The caravan consists of one main room, with bathroom and lavatory leading out of it. The main room is decorated in the Queen Anne style with somewhat severe oak panelling on the walls, relieved with ormolu appliques for candles.'

This contraption was made in England. By removing any trace of danger or hardship it must have succeeded in making even tiger-shooting boring. It is fair to add that it was not usual or typical in its day —any more than the bored faces in plate 23 were typical of Edwardian England as a whole.

26 & 27 Two faces of an Edwardian coal-strike: Published in March, 1912, the pictures show: 'Fifteen passengers in excess of the regulation number carried in an LCC tram car; a stern rule broken by permission in view of a restricted service'; and 'The poor picking colliery rubbish heaps in South Wales in a search for scraps of coal during hard times'. Once again it is interesting to notice that in the latter picture the *ILN* artist, in this case John E. Sutcliffe, has made his drawing sympathetic to the miners. The women are clearly most 'respectable', and the central figure is carrying her coal in what had been a spotless white apron.

Woman's changing role

Edwardian women liked to proclaim that they were liberating themselves from the shackles of Victorianism, and the newspapers and magazines of the day were in the habit of telling them that this was so, presumably because it was thought to promote the sales of newspapers and magazines. The truth in the relationship between the sexes was, no doubt, much the same as it has always been: some women liked to give the impression that they were bossing their men about; others knew that they could get their own way more effectively by not trying to, or at least by not appearing to. None the less, this was the era when women determined to get the vote, though they did not finally get it until 1918. So it is interesting to look through some of the social commentaries of the Edwardian years, and see whether much has really changed, seventy years later.

THE ENGLISH WIFE.

THE AMERICAN HUSBAND.

28 Woman's role on opposite sides of the Atlantic: This drawing of 1903 perhaps makes more of a point now than it did when it was published. After seventy years of the liberation of womanhood the same joke could be published with equal effect today, subject to minor changes in dress and habit.

29 (opposite above) The oppressed Englishwoman of 1905: Mr Punch's view of the subjection of women in the opening years of the century, when the suffragette movement was still in its infancy.

30 (opposite below) Women's Lib, or down with man: At least this drawing in March, 1907, makes the young lady standing in the foreground more attractive to the male eye than were the exponents of Women's Lib in the early 1970s.

PRIMUM VIVERE, DEINDE PHILOSOPHARI.

"Is Florrie's engagement really off, then?"

"Oh, yes. Jack wanted her to give up gambling and smoking, and goodness knows what else."

(Chorus.) "How absurd!!"

Lady (who has asked Jones to tea at her Club). "So awfully sorry. I quite forgot I had a 'Down with Man' Meeting. But please take a seat and make yourself comfortable. We shall only be about an hour."

[Jones says he thinks he'll go and do some shopping.

31

THE SEX QUESTION.
(A STUDY IN BOND STREET.)

32   . . . And by March 1912 women were beginning to take the law into their own hands: A drawing in the *Illustrated London News* records rioting by members of the suffragette movement on the evening of Friday, 1 March, 1912. Shop windows were broken in many parts of the West End, and between £4,000 and £5,000 worth of damage was done—very large sums in those days.

33   Equality of the sexes finally attained (in 1911): If you did not know better, you might easily have supposed that unisex in fashions was a phenomenon only of the early 1970s.

31   Meanwhile harassed men were fighting a hopeless rearguard action at street corners . . .

A changing view of sex

In 1903 most men and women in England probably took what we would call a Victorian view of sex. By 1913 they were beginning to take what we would call a modern view. It is an illusion to suppose that the change took place as a result of the 1914–1918 war. The war did no more than confirm what had already started.

34   Courtship at haymaking: This photograph was probably taken in 1903 or 1904; the place and the characters are unknown. The pitchfork and hay-rake on the man's shoulder suggest that he is on his way to or from haymaking, though I cannot guess the reason for the coiled ropes hanging from the handles. The man, at least, must have known that he was being photographed, but everything about the picture, including the cows grazing the verges, gives the impression that the scene is unposed. In fact it seems to sum up the whole of the man–woman relationship set against the background of the English countryside, the theme on which Thomas Hardy based most of his novels, and which he summed up in the lines:

> *Yonder a maid and her wight*
> *Come whispering by:*
> *War's annals will cloud into night*
> *Ere their story die.*

35   Courtship at the opening of the twentieth century: Talking outside Christmas Cottage, Odiham, Hampshire, about the year 1904, are James Sword, the local church organist, and Miss Budden, who lived at Christmas Cottage. Miss Budden's father was the Odiham-Reading-Basingstoke carrier; he went about the district in a covered van pulled by one horse. Jimmy Sword, I am told, paid court to Miss Budden, but he went away and did not marry her.

36 Sex in advertising—1907 version: The young lady's bathrobe is surely discreet enough by any standard, but the quotation from Coleridge must have bordered on the daring in this context:

> Her gentle limbs did she undress,
> And lay down in her loveliness.

HOW I ENLARGED MY BUST SIX INCHES IN THIRTY DAYS.

AFTER I HAD TRIED PILLS, MASSAGE, WOODEN CUPS, & VARIOUS ADVERTISED PREPARATIONS WITHOUT THE SLIGHTEST RESULTS.

A Simple, Easy Method which any Lady can use at home and quickly obtain a Large and Beautiful Bust.

BY MARGARETTE MERLAIN.

Well do I know the horrors and intense humiliation of being flat-chested ; of having the face of a woman set on the form of a man, and I cannot find words to tell you how good I felt, and what a terrible load was lifted off my mind when I first saw my bust had really grown six inches in size. I felt like a new being, for with no bust I realised I was neither a man nor a woman, but just a sort of creature half-way between.

own. I had been imposed on by charlatans and frauds, who sold me all sorts of pills and appliances for enlarging my bust, but which did me no good whatever. I therefore determined my unfortunate sisters should no longer be robbed by those " fakirs " and frauds, and I wish to warn all women against them.

The discovery of the simple process with which I enlarged my bust six inches in thirty days was

Keep this picture and see your own bust undergoing the same marvellous transformation.

With what pity must every man look at every woman who presents to him a flat chest—a chest like his own. Can such a woman inspire in a man those feelings and emotions which can only be inspired by a real and true woman, a woman with a beautiful well-rounded bust ? Most certainly not.

The very men who shunned me, and even the very women who passed me carelessly by when I was so horribly flat-chested and had no bust, became my most ardent admirers shortly after I obtained such a wonderful enlargement of my bust. I therefore determined that all women who were flat-chested should profit by my accidental discovery, and have a bust like my

due solely to a lucky accident, which I believe was brought about by Divine Providence, and as Providence was good to give me the means to obtain a beautiful bust, I feel I should give my secret to all my sisters who need it. Merely enclose one penny stamp for reply, and I will send you particulars by return post.

I will positively guarantee that any lady can obtain a wonderful enlargement in her bust in thirty days' time, and that she can easily use this process in the privacy of her own house without the knowledge of anyone.—Address, Margarette Merlain (Dept. 885A), 85, Great Portland Street, London, W.

37 Optimism in advertising—1907 version: Magazine advertisements of the period relied frequently on claims that might have been difficult to sustain if they had been tested in a court of law. This one was by no means unusual in its day. The magazines were also widely supported by firms who offered such commodities as 'free phosphorous' by means of which, one advertiser claimed, those suffering from failure of physical and mental vigour, and prematurely old, 'have been restored to a most vigorous and perfectly healthy state. . .the countenance becomes clear and ruddy, the eyes bright, sight improved, deafness overcome, the hair becomes abundant, the step and gait again elastic and determined, the spirits high and generous, the temper cheerful, the love of song and harmony returned'. There was also a much respected advertiser who claimed to 'make men of men and women of women', and appears to have done rather well out of it.

BUSY WIFE, *at the Tele-phone*: "Are you there? Is that you, Harry? Have you taken your 'Wincarnis'? I've just had mine, and you know how anxious I am about you; the Doctor warned me to remind you every day."

'TWIXT LOVE AND DUTY.

BUSY HUSBAND: "Yes, dear! What a good little soul you are! You'll be pleased to know that I have just had my regulation glass, and feel all the better. I must thank the Doctor for pre-scribing such a delicious tonic."

38   The commuter and his wife in 1907: The interesting thing about this charming advertisement is that it appeared in *Country Life*, whose readers were presumably thought by advertisers to be at least less gullible than some. The dialogue records the curious Edwardian habit of beginning a telephone conversation with 'Are you there?' Notice the disarming innocence of the two vertical strips down the middle of the picture to indicate that the wife was in the country and the husband at Ludgate Circus.

39   Not exactly naked, but almost unashamed: The rapidly changing attitude to the human body is shown by this drawing from *Punch* of August 1912. By then, even so reticent a person as Mr Punch had begun to feel that it was all right to indicate that women had bodies under their clothes; though perhaps it was not entirely chance that made Lewis Baumer, who drew the picture, make the young lady in the old-fashioned bathing dress look more feminine than her friend in the more revealing garment.

Lady (coming from the sea). "OH! EXCUSE ME—YOU PROBABLY DON'T KNOW, AS YOU'VE ONLY JUST ARRIVED—BUT, ACCORDING TO THE REGULATIONS OF THIS SILLY PLACE, YOU MUSTN'T WALK ACROSS THE BEACH WITHOUT A GARMENT THAT COVERS YOU FROM HEAD TO FOOT."

Parents and children

The photographs and drawings in this section were made before English parents had taken to reading books on child psychology. Edwardian children were not brought up by the book, or by the light of nature, but according to the way their parents had been brought up. The rules of conduct, for children as well as for grown-ups, were well-known and clearly defined. Not only did the home itself feel secure and permanent; those desirable qualities extended, for most Edwardian children, to the whole of the world outside.

40 Father and daughter in a stable world: We do not know the names of the family, or even where the photograph was taken, though the greenhouse will be recognised in plates 13 and 14. The photograph is one of a collection of glass negatives found by Mr and Mrs John Wareham in the loft of their house, presumably left there years before by a gifted photographer. The print itself contains all the information we need concerning the stalwartness of the father's character and of the bond between him and his daughter.

41 When the generation gap meant no more than the gap between grandfather and grand-daughter: Another photograph from the Wareham collection, presumably by the same photographer though apparently in a different suburban garden.

42 Passing the driving test at the age of ten: We do not know how long this little boy had been driving, but judging by the triumphant expression on his face, my guess is that the picture was taken to mark the big day when he was first let loose on the roads.

43 Father and son in a stable world: To an English boy in an average home in 1903, when the drawing was published in the *Boy's Own Paper*, security was a quality taken so much for granted that no one even noticed it was there. Britain was the world's leading power, and only the most perceptive suspected that she might cease to occupy that position. The drawing was published with no comment beyond the title 'A Boy's Own Snuggery'. Father is helping to clean the collector's-piece helmet, which has not yet been priced beyond the reach of a family of moderate means. Notice the importance attached to firearms. At least one of the weapons is meant for use and not for show. In 1903 a country boy would have been familiar with a .22 rifle or a shotgun at an early age. Notice also, alas, the stuffed bird in the cage beyond father's shoulder—a fashion that led to the disappearance of several of our native species.

44 Popular psychology in the parent–child relationship: *Cassell's Household Guide* of 1911 often illustrated its articles with photographs that had been posed for the purpose. This one carried the startling caption: 'Comfort yourself with the sure knowledge that you have been walking in the high places of motherhood'. It illustrates an article which warned mothers: 'As your girl's thoughts begin to turn to love—as turn they certainly will—encourage her to talk of this matter. Do not preach to her, and be extremely careful as to how you warn her against any silly romance; persuade her to the reading of such fiction as George Eliot and Mrs Craik endowed us with; let her dip into *Vanity Fair*, and get from it an inkling of the true ways of the world, and let the haunting passion of *Jane Eyre* thrill her to an appreciation of what is "lovely and of good report" in the way of a 'sex' novel.'

45 Mother-in-law and daughter-in-law in a stable world: Another of the specially posed photographs used in *Cassell's Household Guide* of 1911 to illustrate articles on practical domestic advice. It carries the splendid caption: 'Many mothers-in-law accept it as a great honour to be asked to make a pudding.'

Nanny's world

Because their mothers were too busy, too idle, or for other reasons were unable to look after their children before they reached school age, Nanny was an important and cherished figure in the lives of many Edwardians. Here are a few glimpses of what she and her world were like.

46 Nanny in her own kingdom: Photographs of Edwardian nannies are not uncommon but this, taken in 1904, is the only one I have seen of an Edwardian nanny actually presiding over her nursery, complete with under-nurse. She in fact held her post in one family in Dorset for a period of fifty years—and even that is probably not a record. Anyone who was nanny for that length of time acquired immense authority, much as Queen Victoria acquired great authority by the simple process of reigning for a long time.

47 Nanny as the advertiser saw her: In March, 1904, this advertisement was probably a fair indication of what many nurseries and their occupants were like, including the curly-haired little boy on the right wearing the then ubiquitous sailor-suit. The children and the room have not been idealised for the purposes of salesmanship, but the nanny is improbably young—perhaps to flatter real nannies into approving of this particular brand of cocoa.

Van Houten's Cocoa

The Nursery.

The Nursery is the training ground of the future generation. Whether the manhood and womanhood of the next decade will be physically and mentally healthy and vigorous depends largely upon the manner in which the children are fed. Mothers should therefore remember that there is no beverage equal to Van Houten's Cocoa for promoting health, strength and good digestion. It is rich in food value, easily digested and most economical in use. Its exquisite natural flavor makes it the favourite beverage for old and young alike.

48   Nanny on an industrial scale: There is nothing new in the idea of a firm providing a nursery in order to employ young married women who would otherwise have to stay at home. The photograph, taken in the creche at Pretty's corset factory in Ipswich, also in 1904, has been carefully posed to get as many children as possible within the range of the lens. The remarkable basketwork pram, a cross between a perambulator and a charabanc, must have been an admirable way of allowing one nurse to air a large load of babies.

49   Nannydom reduced to an absurdity: It was probably not accidental that Wallis Mills's drawing, poking fun at the Edwardian family nanny, in this case supported by two under-nurses, appeared in *Punch* in May, 1912, when the long reign of Nanny was drawing to its close.

THE CALL OF THE BLOOD.

Head Nurse (as last resort to baby who won't take his medicine). "BE BRAVE, DARLING! REMEMBER YOU ARE A TALBOT DE THEESPIGNY!"

In service

The Edwardians did disservice to subsequent generations by their treatment of domestic servants. In previous centuries domestic service had been a highly respected employment, and a post in a good family was keenly sought after. In the early years of the twentieth century this changed, largely I suspect because some employers—perhaps because they themselves had only recently reached the position of being employers—treated their servants with a degree of discourtesy, if not contempt, that we today find astonishing and sometimes nauseating. Not surprisingly the servants objected and they—or their children—sought other ways of earning a living, even though the alternative employment might be more monotonous and boring. By the end of the Edwardian era, domestic servants were becoming hard to get.

In the following pages the trend will be seen in the drawings from *Punch*, of which I have only space for a few but which habitually portrayed servants as dim-witted. This was a particularly cruel and senseless form of humour—especially when one remembers that *Punch* was left lying around the house.

50 Domestic staff at The Rectory, Henley, Suffolk, in about 1903: The boy who is carrying the scuttle of coal was probably the boot boy, and no doubt also helped the gardener. One glance at the good lady behind him is enough to tell us that she worked in a happy household and was a much respected employee who set herself high standards.

51   A gossip at the pump, 1903: The photograph has come to me with no indication of where it was taken; if the pump is still standing, perhaps someone may recognise the house. The cleanness and spruceness of the pretty girl on the right, compared with her companion, is no reflection on the latter. It probably means that she was a parlourmaid, and therefore her work was cleaner than that of her companion, who may well have been the cook.

52   To fetch a pail of water . . . This charming little person was photographed about 1908, evidently in a town. She may have been emptying slops, but I would guess that she was on her way to the pump.

53 Even in 1908 quite a number of town houses still had their own pumps.

Mistress and Maid

Hints on the Training
and Management of
Domestic Servants

I.—For the
Young Mistress

54   The heading for the first of a series of articles in *Cassell's Household Guide* of 1911: When these articles were written, middle-class housewives were already finding it hard to get servants; the writer refers constantly to the Servant Problem, with capital letters. The young mistress, searching for her first servant (only one servant was assumed) was advised to 'write to the clergyman's wife in any parish with which you happen to be familiar, telling her exactly what are your requirements, what wages you propose to give, and asking her if she has any protégée whom she wishes to place in a comfortable situation . . . A girl from the workhouse too, may be rough material, but she is often so willing, and so grateful for small kindnesses, that it is well worth while taking her in hand'.

55   An early version of the vacuum cleaner, 1907: Note that it could be worked either by electric power or by hand, presumably with another servant to work a pump, though that is not clear from the picture. The Aspirator, we are assured, is 'not an experiment but a proved success'.

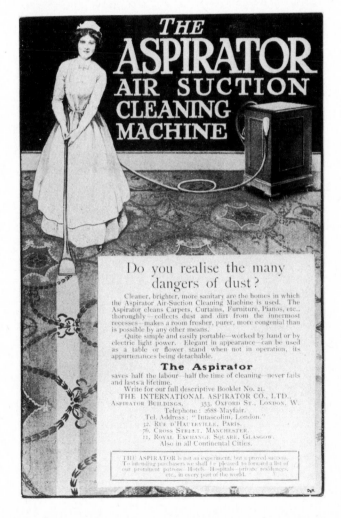

56 Refreshment for the unexpected guests: Another sidelight on social custom in a cocoa advertisement of 1904; see also plate 47. The ritual appears to be that the hostess pours out the cup of cocoa as part of her hospitable duty, but the maid hands it to the visitor on a tray, with the milk and the sugar. The presence of servants was often no more than ceremonial; it would have been just as easy for the hostess to pass the cup herself.

57 *Punch's* contribution to the servant problem, 14 September, 1904: The drawing is from the distinguished pen of Bernard Partridge; but the joke —or attempt at a joke—strikes the present-day reader as distasteful and cruel. Young girls like Belinda could read, and *Punch* was frequently to be found in the houses where they worked.

"THE DESIRE OF THE MOTH FOR THE STAR."

Mistress. "AND YOU DARE TO TELL ME, BELINDA, THAT YOU HAVE ACTUALLY ANSWERED A *Theatrical Advertisement?* HOW *could* YOU BE SUCH A *wicked* GIRL?"

Belinda (whimpering). "WELL MUM,—*other* YOUNG LIDIES—GOW ON THE—STIGE—WHY SHOULDN'T *I* GOW?"

A LITTLE HORTICULTURE IS A DANGEROUS THING.

Squire's Daughter (to Gardener's Wife, who suffers from chronic rheumatism). "Have you tried Swedish Massage, Mrs Brown?"
Mrs. Brown. "I have heard say it be very good for the Rheumatics, Miss; but we don't grow it in these parts."

58 *Punch* in the same vein, but with a lighter touch; 4 January, 1905: Cecil Aldin, an equally distinguished artist, contributed the drawing though he may not have devised the joke. The implication continues to be that servants (or their wives) are mildly imbecilic and that their employers think it funny.

59 & 60 (overleaf) The mood begins to change . . . Wallis Mills in *Punch* on 20 February, 1907 and R. Pegram on 15 April, 1908. Perhaps because servants were becoming harder to get, *Punch's* jokes about servants are slightly less acid as the decade advances. In both of these, one is not quite certain whether it is the servant or her mistress at whom one is laughing.

Lady meeting servant whom she had recommended for a situation. "I am glad to hear that you are getting on so well in your new place. Your employer is a nice lady, and you cannot do too much for her."
Servant (innocently). "I don't mean to, Ma'am."

ANYTHING TO OBLIGE.

"VERY WELL. I ENGAGE YOU AS HOUSEMAID. ER—HAVE YOU ANY FOLLOWERS?"
"NO, 'M; BUT I CAN SOON GET SOME."

Mistress. "OH, BY THE WAY, SMITHERS, I'VE ARRANGED FOR THE BREAKFAST IN THE SERVANTS' HALL TO BE A QUARTER-OF-AN-HOUR EARLIER IN FUTURE."
Smithers. "THEN, MY LADY, I BEG LEAVE TO GIVE NOTICE."
Mistress. "INDEED! WHY?"
Smithers. "WELL, MY LADY, IT SEEMS TO ME THAT THIS ESTABLISHMENT IS BEING CONDUCTED FOR YOUR CONVENIENCE RATHER THAN FOR THAT OF THE SERVANTS."

61 . . . And by 23 April, 1913, the attitude has changed entirely: A convincing drawing by another distinguished *Punch* artist, Lewis Baumer, leaves no doubt as to whose star is in the ascendant. Compare George Belcher's joke in plate 18.

In school

Readers of my previous picture books have pointed out that in neither of them did I pay adequate attention to schools. The omission was not because I did not think the subject interesting or important, but because I had not been able to obtain good photographs taken in the classroom. In spite of much searching, I began to suspect that photographs of real quality did not exist. Happily, in the early years of the century there was in Oxfordshire one of Her Majesty's Inspector of schools (a member of that distinguished body generally known as HMIs) who was an enthusiastic amateur photographer. When he went round from village to village he not only made the proper reports and filled in the proper forms; he also took some wonderfully informative photographs of the children in the classrooms. I am indebted to the Oxfordshire County Education Officer for permission to reproduce some of them here. They provide an interesting comparison with photographs taken in the town schools, and in what we now call the 'private sector', during the same period.

When the photographs were taken, compulsory elementary education was already well-established, and had been free since 1891. Nevertheless the Edwardians were worried that rival nations were paying more attention to public education and to the health and welfare of schoolchildren. In 1906 and 1907 Acts were passed that authorised local authorities to arrange for school meals and for school medical inspection, an important step forward in recognising the State's responsibility in matters that the Victorians would have considered solely a family concern.

A lively account of the visit of an HMI to a country school will be found in Flora Thompson's *Lark Rise*: 'There was no singing or quarrelling on the way to school that morning. The children, in clean pinafores and well-blackened boots, walked deep in thought; or, with open spelling or table books in hand, tried to make up in an hour for all their wasted yesterdays'.

62 Chipping Norton Council Girls' and Infants' School, 7 February, 1906: At the beginning of the century there were more Church Schools of various denominations than there were Board Schools or Council Schools, but an HMI was responsible for inspecting all of them, which explains why both kinds appear in these photographs. The hackney cab waiting outside Chipping Norton school has presumably brought the Inspector from the station.

65 (opposite) East Addington C of E Infants' School, 2 June, 1906: I have not got a copy of HMI's report on this occasion, but one gets the impression that the schoolmistress did not have things so completely under control. There is a wide range of pictures, but no one has managed to get them straight even for inspection. All four of the little girls have white pinafores.

63   South Newington Church of England School, 10 May, 1907: This must surely rank among the finest school photographs taken for the information it provides about what the staff, the children and the buildings were like. Equipment seems to be quite good; there is no lack of maps. There is plenty of daylight, but the three hanging oil lamps would not have given much light by modern standards. For a village school the children are remarkably well turned out, and all the boys are wearing starched Eton collars—perhaps a special effort for the benefit of the Inspector.

64   Ipsden Stoke Church of England School, 19 March, 1907: It is interesting to compare the photograph with the description in HMI's report. 'The school is a brick building with tiled roof. It contains two rooms which are separated by a wood and glass partition. There is one cloakroom and the earth closets are very near the school . . . No drinking conveniences except an old tin. Water drawn from well in back garden—shallow and surrounded by cabbages. A grass playground said to be pretty wet. It is across a road along which motors pass.' Even at that early date, crossing a road with cars on it was regarded as a problem.

66 (opposite) Idbury and Fifield C of E School, 24 August, 1906: We have no information as to why HMI took this particular photograph; it is different from his other photographs in that it shows a classroom with only one child (and teacher's bicycle) left in it. My guess, though it is no more than a guess, is that the girl was being kept in after school.

67 A London school of the same period: Byron Street School, in the East End of London, 1910. We do not know who took this photograph, but it is more posed than the preceding pictures and the standing children have been ranged round the walls in order to get them in. None of the faces looks ill-nourished, but the general impression is that the children are neither as well-dressed nor as happy as their country cousins. The classroom, however, shows more signs of teaching activity, with examples of the children's work pinned on to the walls. I am puzzled by the bucket and spade and the ball and racquet hanging at the back of the class. Confiscated? Or school property for use on demand?

68 Hackney Downs Secondary School handicrafts class, 15 June, 1911: In the Edwardian years public secondary education was still hopelessly inadequate to enable Britain to maintain her place in competition with the rising industrial powers. Only a small proportion of working-class children made their way up through the Edwardian secondary schools; it was the lower-middle-class that benefited from the new opportunities. Donald Read, in *Edwardian England*, points out that 'Of boys born in the years 1910–29, still only one fifth reached secondary school, and middle-class children were four times more likely than working-class children to figure among this number.' There is a general impression of middle-class prosperity about all the boys in this very interesting photograph. The tragedy of the picture, when one thinks about it, is that if these boys were 13 in 1911, they would have reached the age of 19 by 1917—in plenty of time for the slaughterhouse of the Great War.

69 The lighter side of school life: All we know about this charming photograph is that it was taken in the early years of the century, evidently in the playground of a town school.

70 Nursery into schoolroom: When the children of middle- and upper-middle-class families were old enough to escape from the authority of Nanny, they were liable to find themselves in the clutches of a governess; and the nursery, if there were no younger brothers and sisters, would be upgraded to the schoolroom. From that purgatory the boys could escape as soon as they were old enough to go to boarding school. Their sisters might have to stay in the schoolroom until their early teens, though they might be joined by the daughters of one or two neighbouring families who came in to share their lessons.

Out of school

It is often said that children are the same in all ages and play the same kind of games. In fact it is not true, though it may have been true until the very period with which this book is concerned. There is a marked difference between the means by which children in the Edwardian years filled their out-of-school hours and those by which today's children do so. Before 1914 children took it as a matter of course that they would find their own ways of filling their free time; modern children have grown up to expect that much of their leisure will be spent in a passive role, in which entertainment is provided for them. This is partly due to the impact of television, but it began before television sets became widely owned. It is a significant social change, and I suspect that we do not yet understand why it has happened.

73   The heyday of the Eton collar: These village schoolboys in about 1903 may have been wearing their Eton collars, in spite of otherwise somewhat worn clothing, for the benefit of one of the dreaded HMIs referred to in the preceding section, but I doubt it. More probably, their mothers considered that if they wore stiff white collars they were properly dressed, though their trousers might be out at the knees and their stockings beyond darning. The Eton collar, visually as well as morally, was a direct survival of the Puritan strain in the English character. When it was worn out and too tight—and for most boys it inevitably acquired both those qualities with the passage of time—it felt to the wearer like a closely-fitting hacksaw blade. If ever we start dressing boys in Eton collars again, we shall know that another Puritan age is on its way.

71 The great day arrives: Those who have written books about their Edwardian schooldays, or who have included chapters about them in their autobiographies, seem generally to have been those who enjoyed boarding school least. Boys were probably more pleased to go to boarding school then than they are now, if only because it meant escape from the tedium of the schoolroom. This drawing from the *Boy's Own Paper* of 22 July, 1905, shows boys coming home from school and is captioned 'Home for the holiday—Waterloo Station'. It dispels yet another illusion beloved of film producers, television producers and novelists: that the wealthier Edwardian parents neglected their offspring. Notice that these boys are being met not only by one parent but by both mother and father. A picture of a similar train arriving at Waterloo Station in the 1970s would look very different; few fathers would be able to find the time to get away from their desks. Presumably Edwardian fathers found it easier to leave someone else to carry on at the office. I am puzzled by the uniformed nurse-figure on the extreme right. Was she a kind of matron provided by the railway to meet the smaller boys whose parents could not come, and to help the children change trains if necessary? I doubt whether small boys could have been met by their own family Nanny without much ragging from their contemporaries. This picture is yet another example of the care and detail that went into magazine drawings of the period.

72 The lighter side of boarding-school life: Another piece of photographic evidence to belie the popular impression that life in Edwardian boarding schools ranged from the rugged to the barbaric. The four boys are at Lancing College and are having tea with the wife of one of the masters. I do not know the date, but would guess 1905, because the master's wife is wearing a hat almost identical with that worn by the mother in the foreground of plate 71.

74 & 75 Marbles: the fashionable game for all country occasions: Marbles is said to be one of the oldest games to have been played by the human race, and it has presumably been enjoyed without a break until very recently. The equipment, after all, is within the reach of any child who can roll pellets out of clay, though the boys in these two photographs were probably playing with the more sophisticated glass marbles. But whatever has become of the game in the 1970s? Perhaps, like so much else, its disappearance after countless centuries can be blamed on the motor car. Modern children would not survive long if they used the same lanes in the same way today.

76 The season for water sports: We have no record of where this photograph was taken, but the scene must have repeated itself in high summer all over England during the early years of the century. Notice how well maintained the edge of the pond is by modern standards. In horse-drawn days a village pond was functional and not merely attractive: horses and carts were regularly driven into the water in hot, dry weather. Writing some thirty or forty years before this photograph was taken, Richard Jefferies referred to the risk of drowning that was run by village children playing unobserved in streams and ponds. The traffic hazard, to modern mothers, has become so acute and all pervasive that the risk of ponds seems negligible by comparison.

77 Coastal craft in the days of sail: The idea that children should play on the beach in summer is so well established that one might suppose that it had been going on for centuries; yet it was only about 100 years before this photograph was taken that seaside holidays became fashionable. The great grandmothers of these little girls no doubt played by the sea as they are doing; but if their more remote ancestors did the same thing, they have left little record of it; the beach was no more a playground than were the mountains or the snowfields.

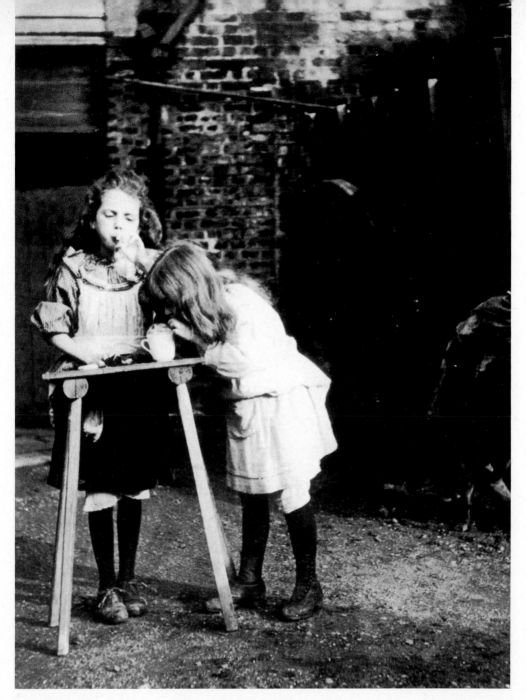

78   One of the more attractive aspects of soap and water: We all know that bubble-blowing as a sport flourished in the 1880s, when Millais painted his famous picture, but it would be interesting to know when children first discovered soap bubbles. Not all that long ago, I would guess; I doubt whether earlier soaps provided the right surface-tension. The little girl on the right, incidentally, is a reminder of what children had to put up with before the days of rubber wellingtons. This child had 20 boot buttons; almost impossible with cold fingers, and difficult even with the aid of the special tool for the job, the button-hook.

Old age but new hope

Since there was a section on old age in both my previous books, it may well be asked what more can be said here. I have, however, put in this short section to reinforce a point that I have already made in the foreword: the years 1903–1913 were not only years of great social progress in a general sense; they saw the introduction of State Old Age Pensions as a right and not as a charity. In 1909 pensions became payable at the age of 70, though only those whose income did not already exceed £21 a year received the full pension. Moreover, a pensioner was not eligible if he had 'habitually failed to work according to his ability, opportunity and need,' or if he had been in prison within the previous ten years. Nevertheless even this limited measure was a great success. In 1909 over 400,000 pensions were distributed in England and Wales to nearly 45 per cent of the population aged over 70. Moreover, the Act expressly stated that receipt of an Old Age Pension would not 'deprive the pensioner of any right, franchise or privilege'.

79 The age of anxiety—1903: However hard a man worked during his active years, and however carefully he tried to save, there came a time when his earning powers diminished and he could look forward to the future only with dread. The worst thing that could happen to self-respecting men or women was that they would end their days in the workhouse, and the horror of it filled the minds of the poor as old age approached. To escape the workhouse you did not simply have to be frugal and industrious; you also needed to be lucky. All the anxiety of old age in 1903, before the introduction of the first statutory Old Age Pension, has been preserved in this study of an unknown man by an unknown photographer.

80 When unemployment and old age were joint problems: After the introduction of Old Age Pensions in 1909, both Churchill and Lloyd George recognised that the next social problem that had to be tackled was unemployment. It had become realised at last that a good man might be unemployed without its being in any way his own fault. The young Churchill referred movingly to the casual labourer 'who is lucky to get three or at the outside four days' work in the week, who may often be out of a job for three or four weeks at a time, who in bad times goes under altogether, and who in good times has no hope of security and no incentive to thrift, whose whole life and the lives of his wife and children are embarked in a sort of blind, desperate, fatalistic gamble with circumstances beyond his comprehension or control'. Churchill's Labour Exchanges Act of 1909 assumed that the problem of unemployment rested largely with the employers. The pathetic thing about this fine-looking and carefully-groomed old man, selling matches and collar studs, is that he was almost certainly, in 1913, too old to get a new job and too young for the Old Age Pension.

81 *Punch* takes a look at the introduction of old age pensions: The caption to this drawing of 1909 refers to the stipulation, when pensions were first introduced, that a State Old Age Pensioner should not have been in prison within the previous ten years.

SWEET MEMORIES.
Pension Enquiry Officer. "Have you ever been in the hands of the police?"
Applicant. "Well—er—sir, you see I used to be a cook! Girls will be girls! Besides, it was a good many years ago, and he was a sergeant!"

Social security

Among the most valuable forms of social security that the Edwardians enjoyed was the security provided by the constabulary. There were plenty of policemen for the work that had to be done, and there was usually one to be found standing on the street corner just at the moment when he was needed. It had not always been so, as some of the older Edwardians could remember. An incident in Trollope's *The Prime Minister* makes it clear that for the Victorians it was frightening but not altogether unexpected to be waylaid by thieves in London's parks in the dark. And in Hardy's *Return of the Native* Captain Vye, who lived in the country, kept a pair of loaded pistols over his bed. As the following photographs and drawings suggest, the Edwardians regarded the omnipresent policeman with a certain degree of amusement, but always with affection and esteem.

82   The policeman on the bridge—as the camera saw him: The photograph is undated but comes, I would guess, from the earliest years of the Edwardian era. It has the merit of being unposed, and it shows the archetypal London bobby: large, benign, sociable when occasion offered, but awe-inspiring to those of evil intent.

83 The policeman on the bridge—as the artist saw him: This drawing appeared in the *Boy's Own Paper* of 9 May, 1903, with the title 'Lost in London'. It was, I imagine, intended by the editor to reassure his younger readers that all would be well if they were so unfortunate as to get lost in the great city; and the artist has assumed, probably correctly in his day, that a policeman would be sure to turn up within a moment or two if ever one were needed.

84 'Awkward—very!' Another drawing from the *Boy's Own Paper*, dated 16 July, 1904. It is interesting both because it presupposes the ubiquity of policemen in 1904, even in remote places in the country, and because the artist's impression of the archetypal policeman's back view exactly corresponds with that of the camera in plate 82.

ARMS AND THE ——.

Mrs. Flanagan. "WELL, I SUPPOSE WE'LL SOON BE HAVING POLICEWOMEN, AND THEN YOU'LL BE OUT OF A JOB."

P.C. Flanagan. "NO, MY DEAR, I FANCY YE'LL FIND THE STHRONG ARM OF THE LAW WILL ALWAYS BE WEARIN' THE THROUSERS!"

85 An Edwardian preview of the policewoman: A joke from *Punch* of 10 April, 1907, which, like all H. M. Brock's drawings, is full of interesting detail. The policeman's kitchen is solidly but well furnished, and there is a clean cloth on the table with the laundry folds still showing; this was before the days of inflation, when a policeman's job was secure and well-paid. The cottage loaf is mouth-watering to those who can remember that product of the village baker. Mr Flanagan would have been startled had he been able to guess what the contents of his dresser shelves and mantelshelf would be fetching in antique shops 70 years later.

86 Law enforcement in a Hampshire country town: This photograph, dated about 1908, appears to have been specially taken for publication as a postcard in Odiham in Hampshire. The stocks were no doubt a genuine antiquity, but to our eyes it is remarkable—unless the cast were actors—that the photographer should have been able to persuade not only the 'miscreants' but the entire local police force, five policemen and a sergeant, to come and take part in his charade. The peace and security of Odiham in 1908 must have been inviolable in such stalwart and well-gloved hands.

The national health

All shades of Edwardian political opinion were worried about the state of the nation's health, though for varying reasons: Liberals and radicals on grounds of social conscience; right-wing Conservatives because they feared that if the island race deteriorated the Empire would fall. Both sides had good cause for alarm. The abuses of nineteenth-century industrialism were having a cumulative effect. Seebohm Rowntree's study of urban poverty had shown that between 1897 and 1901 nearly half of the army recruits in York, Leeds and Sheffield were rejected on medical grounds; in 1903 the Director General of the Army Medical Service claimed that six out of every ten Englishmen were unfit for military service. Not far away, over the North Sea, those warlike and aggressive Germans appeared to be noticeably healthier and to have avoided—if only because they had learned by our mistakes—the worst effects of the Industrial Revolution.

87 The village shopkeeper, everyman's medical consultant in 1903: I have included this drawing from *Punch* of 23 December, 1903, not only because of the prominent display of pills on the counter and the little girl's Mum's request for radium which was the fashionable medical miracle of its day, but because of the record that it provides of a village shop seventy years ago. Until recently I could have named half a dozen village shops which were still almost identical to it, but even those survivors have now felt obliged, because of the pressures of competition, to turn themselves into miniature supermarkets.

LATEST CHRISTMAS NOVELTY.

"Please, Mother says, can you let her 'ave a 'arf ounce of this 'ere Radium she 'ave read so much about in the paper?"

73

88 Early days of the health visitor: C. E. Brock's drawing of 27 April, 1904, is carefully vague about the status of the lady visitor; she could be the squire's lady, the parson's lady or a visitor from one of a number of welfare societies of the day. The nurse referred to, however, is clearly the District Nurse, who was a well-established character in the countryside by that date. The Queen Victoria Jubilee Institute, forerunner of the Queen's Institute of District Nursing, was founded in 1887.

Lady Visitor (to old parishioner). "WELL, MR. HUGGINS, AND HAS THE NURSE BEEN TO SEE YOU YET?"
Old Parishioner. "YES, MUM, THANK'EE. SHE'S CALLED ONCE, AN' DONE MY FOOT MORE GOOD THAN ALL THE IMPRECATIONS I'VE EVER USED!"

89 The country doctor in an age of transition: In *Punch* of 25 October, 1911, the unhurrying country doctor has already become a figure of fun. Nevertheless, in 1911 almost all country doctors still made their rounds in the saddle or in a gig; one or two rode bicycles and a few used motor cars, but cars were felt to be unreliable for medical purposes because of their susceptibility to punctures and their refusal to start in cold weather.

Old Doctor (who has been gossiping for three-quarters of an hour). "WELL, WELL, I MUST BE GOING. I'VE GOT TO VISIT AN OLD LADY IN A FIT."

90 (opposite) What the Edwardians were up against: A drawing published in the *Illustrated London News* of 13 January, 1912, when coal was the universal fuel and London fogs were at their worst. The three columns of soot shown alongside the Nelson Column indicate the amount of soot per square mile per year in the City of London, in south-west London and in Sutton, Surrey, respectively. Those who do not remember London in its dirtier days have no realisation of how much we have gained by the Clean Air Acts. Washing stone buildings is now worth while because, once they are clean, they stay clean. In Edwardian London it would have been a waste of time. The comparative cleanliness of Sutton explains the Edwardian preoccupation with country air and, to some extent, the tendency of London to spread out over the countryside in an unavailing effort to escape from the pollution.

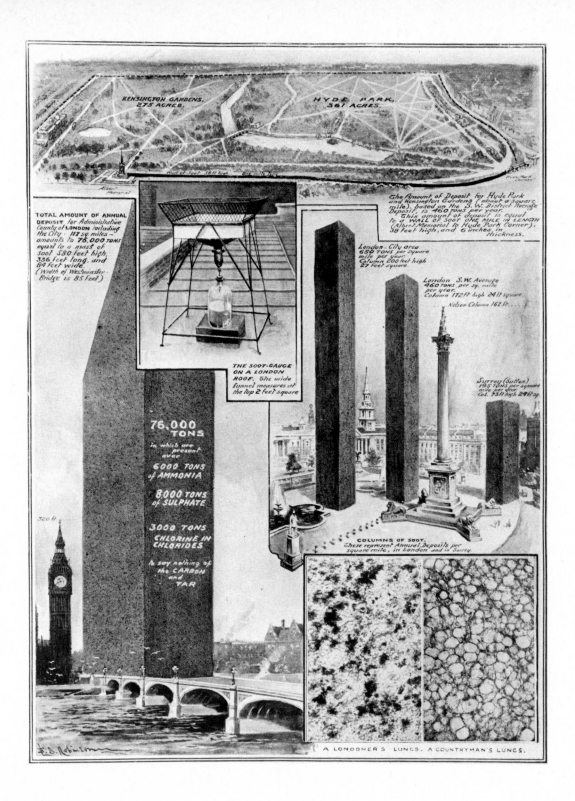

KENSINGTON GARDENS, 275 ACRES.

HYDE PARK, 561 ACRES.

Wall of Soot 38 ft high.

Albert Memorial

Hyde Park Corner

TOTAL AMOUNT OF ANNUAL DEPOSIT for Administrative County of LONDON including the City. 117 sq. miles - amounts to **76,000 TONS** equal to a mass of soot 550 feet high, 336 feet long, and 84 feet wide. (Width of Westminster Bridge is 85 feet.)

The Amount of Deposit for Hyde Park and Kensington Gardens (about a square mile), based on the S.W. District Average Deposit, is 460 tons per year. This amount of deposit is equal to a **WALL OF SOOT ONE MILE IN LENGTH** (Albert Memorial to Hyde Park Corner), 38 feet high, and 6 inches in thickness.

THE SOOT-GAUGE ON A LONDON ROOF. The wide funnel measures at the top 2 feet square.

London - City area 650 TONS per square mile per year. Column 200 feet high 27 feet square.

London S.W. Average 460 TONS per sq. mile per year. Column 172 ft high 24 ft square.

Nelson Column 162 ft.

Surrey (Sutton) 195 tons per square mile per year. Col. 75 ft high 24 ft sq.

76,000 TONS in which are present over

6000 TONS of AMMONIA

8000 TONS of SULPHATE

3000 TONS CHLORINE IN CHLORIDES

to say nothing of the CARBON and TAR

520 ft.

COLUMNS OF SOOT. These represent Annual Deposits per square mile, in London and in Surrey.

A LONDONER'S LUNGS.   A COUNTRYMAN'S LUNGS.

91 Tooth-pulling as part of the fun of the fair: This photograph came to me with no indication of where it was taken, but it has all the appearance of being unposed; certainly tooth-pulling was commonplace at Edwardian country fairs. Because no-one in the United Kingdom need now have a tooth taken out except by a qualified dentist, we are inclined to take qualified dentistry for granted. Seventy years ago the scene in the photograph was thought by children to be worth watching as a sideshow, but it was certainly not unusual. Observe the kind father in the background holding up his little girl so that she can have a good look.

ARTIFICIAL TEETH.

Important Notes by H. H. DREW,

15, Buckwell Street, Plymouth.

Have your teeth examined periodically.
Should tartar collect, have them scaled to prevent decay.
At the first appearance of decay, have it removed, and the tooth filled.
Should they be out of position, have them regulated.
In case of abscess, or inflammation at the roots, and extraction becomes necessary, have it replaced with artificial.

FOR FOOD IS LIFE.

And teeth are the regulators of the food; without teeth, indigestion and numerous other bodily complaints arise.

ALL TEETH EXTRACTED PAINLESS.

Mr. H. H. DREW begs to inform the Public that he has had several years' experience with a most eminent Licentiate of Dental Surgery, London, and four years with Mr. Stephens, and can therefore tender his services with confidence of giving every satisfaction.

Charges strictly Moderate. Consultations Free and all work guaranteed.

92 All teeth extracted painless: Notice that Mr Drew, in this advertisement from *Doidge's Western Counties Illustrated Annual*, does not even claim letters after his name. His qualification for the services he offers is that he has had 'Several years' experience with the most eminent Licentiate of Dental Surgery, London'.

93 Stretching the milk a little: The Edwardian artist's view of an idyllic rural scene calls for no comment except, perhaps, to draw attention to the word on the old gentleman's hatband. HM Inspectors of Foods date from the Public Health Act of 1875, but adulteration of milk with water and starch continued to be prevalent because, with countless independent retail outlets, it was hard to control.

94 Fresh from the kettle: In public parks and similar places a cow tethered by the milk-seller's stall could often be pointed to as evidence of the freshness of the milk (*Punch*, 1907). Perhaps there is something to be said for today's system of milk marketing, even though it has produced a generation of children who think that milk comes out of bottles and who turn up their noses when they first discover its real origin.

THE RED-HOT COW:
"OH, MUMMY, IT'S BURNT ME!"

Time to stand and stare

One of the distinctions between the Edwardian and the Victorian attitude to life was that the Edwardians were rediscovering the importance of leisure. The nineteenth century's puritanical view of the importance of hard work was greatly moderated in the early years of the new century. H.G. Wells's shop assistants, it is true, were overworked, underpaid and frightened of the sack, but at least they knew that this was wrong and that they ought to do something about it. W. H. Davies's *Autobiography of a Super-Tramp*, published in 1908, was symptomatic of the change; the book was a success not merely because Bernard Shaw took it under his wing but because it expressed the Edwardians' private longing to step off the treadmill; it is inconceivable that a similar book published, say, forty years earlier would have been so successful. Even among those who have not read W. H. Davies, he is known today for the lines:

What is this life if full of care,
We have no time to stand and stare?

95 ... And time to sit and drink: Or to sit and think, or just to sit. I do not know the names or history of this impressive couple, or what occasion they are celebrating. The photographer, presumably, was the rightful owner of the third glass of port that is standing, as yet unsipped, on the table. But there can be little doubt that life had used the couple tolerably well. They were—in 1908 when the photograph is believed to have been taken—the loyal and solid subjects of a King-Emperor who ruled over the largest Empire that the world had known, and they comported themselves as befitted such persons.

96   The quiet waters by: This picture was prised for me out of a family album by a member of the family, who tells me that the lady angler was under instruction when the photograph was taken but never became very accomplished with a fly rod. The picture not only preserves the calm and serenity of the time but records that in this family, at least, the new attitude to feminine emancipation was not yet accepted, and modest women did not admit to having legs. One can only hope that her overcoat was designed to withstand the effects of immersion, and that under it she was wearing waterproof waders of the type worn by her instructor in the next photograph.

97   Grayling the quarry? I am indebted for the photograph, and for the one that precedes it, to Major and Mrs George Cree, of Moignes Court, Dorset. When the family album, from which the pictures are taken, was compiled it was assumed that those who looked at the album would know all about everybody in it, so the information is fragmentary and is often no more than the initials of the characters shown. There is a lesson in this for those who compile family albums today: remember the readers of tomorrow.

98 & 99 An anthropomorphic view of animals: The Edwardian public had an inexplicable taste for captive wild animals trained to behave like human beings. The wretched little organ-grinder's monkey, wearing a parody of human clothes and drinking from a bottle, strikes us as pathetic, but it must have drawn coppers into the hat in its day. In *A Country Camera* I included a photograph of a rather mangy-looking dancing bear. The drawing reproduced here, from the *Boy's Own Paper* of 3 September, 1904, is no doubt slightly idealised but seems to us cruel rather than entertaining. When it was published it was captioned 'Strangers in a Strange Land'. The drawing is photographic in manner and may well have been based on a photograph, but it was typical of the *BOP*'s method of presentation: the boy in the foreground, with whom young readers could identify, stands a little apart from the crowd of villagers, so that the crowd forms part of the spectacle. He is wearing what boys of 1904 would have regarded as the latest thing in schoolboy clothes, whereas his grandfather is in the fashion of the 1860s.

100 A popular seaside resort at the climax of the railway age: Weymouth Sands, from the Frith collection. It is typical of the work of the highly professional photographer, who was a specialist in seaside scenes, using a tripod and taking plenty of time to get just the effect he wanted.

101 A view of Swanage, Dorset, also by Frith: Looking north from the quiet resort of Swanage, sustained by a branch railway but not yet overgrown, across an area now covered with buildings towards Ballard Down (mercifully unspoilt in the 1970s). The picture taken within a mile of the railway station, is a reminder of how easy it was for the Edwardian middle-class family to escape from the crowds for a quiet holiday in a clean little town, with unpolluted sea (the sewage problem was too small to be worth worrying about) and miles of almost empty beach. The small figure on the road just approaching White's bathing station is, as one can see with a magnifying glass on the original print, that ubiquitous Edwardian character, a policeman wheeling his bicycle.

MR. LEANDER JONES, WHO IS VERY PARTICULAR ABOUT AQUATIC ETIQUETTE, TAKES A FEW AMERICAN FRIENDS ON THE RIVER, AND WISHES HE HADN'T.

102 The arrival of unprofessional photography: Mr Eastman and his Kodak cameras may have disconcerted the conservative Mr Leander Jones, in this drawing from *Punch* of August, 1905, but the new habit that he introduced made possible the kind of picture in plate 103.

103 The day of the family seaside snapshot: The bathers are unknown, the date is about 1908, and the picture, from the Kodak library, is believed to have been an entry in a snapshot competition of its day.

Any amount of time
to stand and stare

There can be little doubt that tramps in Edwardian England were better off than they have
been at any time since. In the 1920s and 1930s high unemployment meant that many unfortunate men were walking the highways who were not tramps at all, and this must have
spoiled the market for the genuine ones; and since 1945 housewives on whom tramps might
once have relied for support have come to feel that the Welfare State has made private charity
unnecessary. In *The Autobiography of a Super-Tramp*, which I have referred to in the previous
section, W. H. Davies described in detail how easily, from spring to autumn, a tramp could
lead a comfortable existence in the English countryside. This was partly because the less inten-
sive agriculture of those days left nooks and corners where tramps could find comfortable out-
door quarters, and partly because every professional tramp knew of a network of houses
where he could be sure of a decent meal for the asking.

104   The pleasures of a private income without the income: The picture must surely have been posed,
or taken with the agreement of the subject. No self-respecting tramp would have allowed a photographer to creep up on him unawares. But the background against which he has been photographed is
not posed, and it is a good indication of the more casual farming of the day and of the many odd corners
in the countryside where all kinds of wild life, including the human kind, could live in peace and
security. See plate 20 for Mr Punch's view of a tramp of 1908.

Caravan life—the reality

In theory, the law in Edwardian days was not very tolerant towards gypsies, and there were plenty of policemen in the countryside to see that the law was enforced. In reality, however, gypsies and other travellers were less harassed than they are today. The roads were quiet and safe, and the countryside was uncrowded. If van- or tent-dwellers were moved on from one site, they would usually know of several other sites within a day's gentle drive.

105   Travellers without a van: All the photographs that I have seen of Victorian and Edwardian gypsies and other travelling people show that they used tents almost as much as vans; the van-dwellers in the next photograph have both. This family, who were not quite as well off as those in plate 106, probably carried all their goods including the ramshackle tent in the two-wheeled cart, but they are reasonably well shod and none of the children is barefooted. Making clothes pegs appears to be the family's occupation.

106   Van-dwellers on the Dorset downs: The family must have agreed to keep still while the photograph was taken, but I doubt if anything has been deliberately posed or arranged. It is just possible that the woman with the baby on her knee, who also has a hen in her right arm, had scooped the hen up because it was wandering about and being a nuisance. More probably it was in her arms because the family unit included humans and animals on more-or-less equal terms. In the original photograph, studied with a magnifying glass, the hen can be seen to be entirely at ease. It is difficult to assess affluence or poverty in travelling people, then as now, because their standards are different from those of fixed society, but this family appear to be comfortably off within their own terms. Even the little boy with his cap askew is well shod.

Caravan life—the romantic view

By the early years of the century urban escapists were turning to the caravan. On 22 June, 1907, *Country Life* published an article by Bertram Smith, who had spent much time touring in England and Scotland in the caravan shown in plate 107. Even in 1907, however, he preferred to keep to minor roads, where he would be less likely to encounter motor cars; since his caravan took up the full width of the average lane, and the cars of that day had very uncertain brakes, his caution was justified. With a heavy caravan, normally pulled by one horse (though trace horses were obtainable), travelling was hard work at times, especially for the horse. Mr Bertram Smith made elaborate detours to avoid towns, carefully skirting Tunbridge Wells and Sevenoaks, and he warned other would-be caravanners that in the north of Sussex one was already 'stumbling upon the outposts of London and must turn sharply south to avoid those sinister signs of a too dense population—villas and golf links'.

107   An amateur gypsy of 1907: The photograph of Mr Bertram Smith leading his horse was captioned, when it was first published, 'By Shady Ways, if Rough'. Like the real gypsies, Mr Smith carried a small tent into which he could move some of his stores to make more room inside the caravan itself.

108   A caravan for the Church Army: The present-day use of caravans as mobile offices, particularly at agricultural shows and horse shows, dates from the horse-drawn era. No doubt this van was used as living quarters in addition to its function as an information centre, and fairs and shows were among the places where it operated. I would guess that the clergyman who is driving lived in the van. He used two horses, although the van does not look much larger than that in the preceding picture, probably because his load included a heavy stock of books and tracts. The role of his companion with the bicycle is less certain. Did he accompany the van, riding a bicycle to lighten the load on the horses? Or was he the local curate who had come out to greet his itinerant friend?

109   Escape route, 1908: This joke appeared in *Punch* of June, 1908, only one year after the publication of Mr Bertram Smith's article. Even allowing for artist's licence, it seems that the idea of organised caravan parks has an earlier origin than most of us would have guessed. Surprisingly enough, three of the vans in George Morrow's drawing are already motorised.

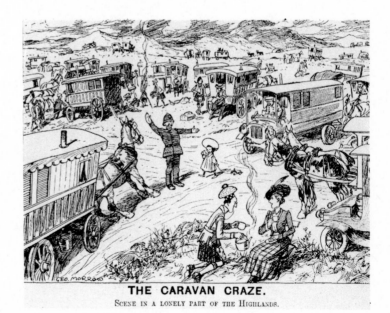

THE CARAVAN CRAZE.
Scene in a lonely part of the Highlands.

Under canvas—the romantic view

It is worth comparing the rosy view of camping in this section with the reality (plate 105) as it seemed to those whose permanent home was in a tent. Camping as an escape from urban civilisation has an older history than caravanning, and the idea of holidays in tents was well-established in Edwardian days. The photographs that follow were lent to me by Mr E. G. Valentine and are taken from an album in which the text was hand-written by his father, in 1913, under the title 'Tales of a Tent'. 'Camping out' we are told, 'is one of the most enjoyable and healthy holidays one can have. Living the simple life with a company of congenial spirits, practically in the open air the whole time, what could be more delightful? Campers are often looked upon as being not quite right in the upper storey, but a week's experience would probably make the scoffer change his opinion.' The camp site was in the Lake District.

110   Rigours of camping in 1913—the baggage train: This cartload contained the equipment and supplies for one week's camping, so the party were doing all they reasonably could to mitigate the hardships of life under canvas. Their standards may perhaps have been acquired from those who had first tasted camp life, either as soldiers or as civilians, in the Indian Empire, where the supply of servants was unlimited. According to Mr Valentine's records, however, these campers did their own manual work. The two boys, one with the inevitable Eton collar, are local onlookers, perhaps hoping to pick up a tip.

111 Rigours of camping in 1913—the tent: The size of the tent can be judged from the group of three men standing on the right. They had headroom even at the sides. It would be interesting to know what it cost to hire such substantial equipment in 1913; Mr Valentine's records do not tell us.

112 Rigours of camping in 1913—the pantry: Mr Valentine's account is filled with details of how he and his companions passed their time and particularly with how often they fell into the lake. I suspect that the writer was an admirer of Jerome K. Jerome and had read *Three Men in a Boat*, but he does not explain where all this equipment came from; my guess is that most of it was supplied by the contractor from whom the party hired their tent. The pantry, incidentally, appears to have been in the A-shaped ridge tent on the left in plate 111.

Behind it all, the land

Before 1914 every Englishman was a landed gentleman—at least in the sense that outside the towns there was what appeared to be an inexhaustible amount of open countryside to which he and his contemporaries could escape when they wanted to. The land was still the permanent background to people's lives; the suburbs seemed no more than a recent and perhaps ephemeral intrusion. The following photographs provide a glimpse of the landscape and the country habit that formed the unchanging elements in the Edwardian scene.

113   Piers Plowman in the opening years of the twentieth century: His plough contains more metal parts than would have been familiar to most of his forebears who ploughed English fields, but the craft that he followed would have been familiar to all of them. He and his horses have carried their mid-day meal into the autumn fields and are enjoying it in the time-honoured manner, in silent companionship.

114 Returning the fertility to the soil: When this picture was published in *Country Life* on 18 November, 1905, it bore the title 'Out in the Vields a Carrin' Dung' and illustrated an article on the shortage of manure; this some seventy years before our present-day shortage of imported fertilisers. By the beginning of the twentieth century, agriculture had recovered from the worst effects of nineteenth-century depression; the agricultural population had not merely stabilised at somewhere round one million but was actually increasing towards 1,250,000.

115 Bringing home the last load of hay . . . The composition of this 1903 photograph was at least partly contrived, and the clouds may well have been added afterwards. But the peaceful character of the countryside that it records was genuine, and in its day appeared immutable. By today's standards towns were small, and the countryside extended for untold acres.

116   . . . And the last load of corn: By C. W. Teager, a photographer of the Essex countryside in the Edwardian era. In the field behind the waggon is the stubble of a crop that has been sown with a drill; it has probably been harvested with a reaper-binder, then stooked by hand and loaded manually on to the waggon. To modern eyes the load pulled by a single horse still seems astonishing; in addition to the crop there are two men on top of the load to hold it down, and there seems to be enough spare horse-power for the farmer's son to enjoy a ride as well. The woman in the foreground, with food and drink for the harvesters, is no doubt the farmer's wife.

117 & 118 (overleaf)   Loading and stacking wheat in Sussex, with a team of oxen: The two pictures were taken in about 1903, but not at the same place. Plate 117 shows Housedean farm, near Lewes, and Plate 118 Lades farm, near Falmer. Of the latter photograph, the Museum of English Rural Life tell me that when the owner died the heirs sold the farm and the new man gave up oxen. It is reasonable to wonder whether, when the oil runs out, oxen and heavy horses will again be found to be economic. Oxen were used to work English fields from Roman times and earlier, though I have never understood the arithmetic that made them viable compared with horses. Six oxen appear to be needed for a load that could have been managed by one or perhaps two horses.

119 Mr Richardson, the ox-man at Lades farm: Mr Richardson was born at Falmer, near Brighton, and spent his whole life in the same locality. He worked for thirty-eight years at Lades farm, handling the teams of oxen, one of which is seen in the preceding photograph.

120 The molecatcher: Among the photographic records of nineteenth- and early twentieth-century country craftsmen, molecatchers seem to be disproportionately prominent. Perhaps they were easily recognisable and attracted photographers' attention more often than some of the others.

121 Gran Girdler, of West Street, Odiham, busy with her washing: Her grandchildren, I am told, still live in the same part of Hampshire. Her husband worked for a Mr Smith, of Odiham, who owned a number of traction engines and hired them out for such contract work as threshing. The boilers of Mr Smith's engines were used to heat the water for the celebration tea held in Odiham for the Diamond Jubilee of Queen Victoria.

Evil communications
corrupt good manners

Of all the changes that have ever been made in the English countryside, one of the greatest was caused by the motor car, and it took place during the ten years with which this book is concerned. In 1903 the roads, in town and country alike, were peaceful and safe for those who used them, including those on foot; yet by 1913 that paradise was lost, and all the evils of which we now complain were familiar subjects for jokes or anger. I have chosen the pictures in this section because they show at a glance the peace and security that we have forfeited, and the irrevocability and suddenness with which the change took place.

122   A group of road users near Wareham, in Dorset, in the early years of the century: If a pedestrian or horseman happened to come by, he threaded his way among the cows, and neither party was in the least inconvenienced. If someone came along in a gig or a waggon, the cows would move gently over to let him through. Only the dust was disturbed.

123   Paradise lost: Outside the post office at East Lulworth in Dorset. It is hard to believe, now, that the photograph was taken in real life and not in a dream: that people actually lived in villages all over England in this kind of quiet and serenity. Here was the countryside that Rupert Brooke and his contemporaries wrote about; to many Englishmen, a few years later, it was what they fought for. Life in English villages must have been like this not merely briefly, in the Golden Years of the early Edwardian era, but for many centuries, before private individual transport somehow became hopelessly at odds with private individual happiness.

124 A lift home from school: It wasn't actually necessary to take the pony through the pond; there was plenty of road over towards the cottage. But on a warm day in early spring the pony liked it because he could stop for a drink, and it was good for the wheels because it prevented the spokes from drying out and working loose.

125　West Street, Bridport, Dorset: Of the road-users in the photograph, eight of them—six boys and two men—are just standing and staring. In 1904 that was in no way unusual; it is only to our traffic-conditioned eyes that it looks odd. Even in the 1930s it was a characteristic of market towns that the inhabitants liked walking about in the middle of the road. By now they have learnt not to, and those who didn't learn have died out.

126   The Old Coach Road, Edgware: When the photograph was reproduced in *Country Life* of 23 May, 1903, the scene would have been considered one of considerable bustle and activity. The coach roads were so little used that taxpayers were constantly complaining of the unnecessary expense of keeping them up.

127 Traffic control outside the Crown Hotel, Woodbridge, Suffolk: The man with the flag is Mr Horace Reynolds. When motor cars first began to appear in the streets of Woodbridge Mr Reynolds, like most of his fellow townsmen, was aware of the danger that they caused to pedestrians and to horse-drawn traffic. Unlike his fellow townsmen, however, Mr Reynolds did something about it. Voluntarily and without pay, he took on the task of controlling traffic at this dangerous corner with a red flag. When he died, in 1910, the townsmen put up a stone with the following inscription:

TO
THE MEMORY OF
HORACE REYNOLDS,
(POLL)
WHO DIED 22nd. AUGUST, 1910
AGED 32 YEARS

Though lacking learning, or wealth, yet by
his self-imposed task of watching over the
motor and other traffic at the cross corner
in this town, in the course of his duty pre-
venting many serious mishaps, he proved
himself a true helper of his fellow men, and
daily earned the gratitude not only of the
townsfolk, but also of all motorists and
others who passed through the town.

128   When the bicycle was king: For one brief period, when minor roads were metalled but not yet tarred, and motor cars were hardly seen, the bicycle was king. It could go further and faster than any horse-drawn vehicle could travel without a change of horses, and it was silent and safe. A remarkable piece of evidence of the safety of the roads in the early years of this century is provided by an article in *The Boys' Own Paper* of 26 May, 1906. This is an account, evidently written for schoolboys to emulate, of a solo ride from London to the south coast on a frosty winter night. The writer set out at dusk. 'You have three or four miles to go before you reach the outskirts of town, three or four miles of roads more or less indifferent, of shop lamps and street lamps, of flaring naptha lamps upon the coster's barrows, of a multitude of lights moving hither and thither upon all kinds of vehicles.' The author complains of cold hands and feet in the frosty weather, and continues with an account of a slow ride out through the suburbs, among trams and vans. Finally he gets free of the built-up zone.

'Now your ride has commenced, and the darkness gives you an involuntary thrill, for your eyes are still blinded by the light of the town you have left behind. When your eyes have become accustomed somewhat to the darkness they wander to the ground, and you dimly see the luminous circle cast by your lamp. You are not quite sure where the road is. You know, of course, that it is somewhere beneath you, but you are by no means sure upon which side you are riding. . . After running into the side of the road a few times more or less gently, your eyes become accustomed to the darkness and you recover your self-confidence.' The ride that the author describes takes him through Caterham and Godstone to East Grinstead, then south through Ashdown Forest and the South Downs to the coast at Newhaven. What, I wonder, would be the chances of survival of any schoolboy who attempted the same ride on a wintry night now?

129 The motorway builders: They may not have been building a motorway in the modern sense of the term, but they were in the eyes of their contemporaries when this photograph was taken at Crondall, Surrey. They were tarring the road so that it would be less muddy in winter and less dusty in summer, so providing a suitable surface for the increasing numbers of motor cars.

130 A turning point in the struggle between car and horse: In the opening years of the century, most people thought that the motor car was no more than a fad of the rich and that it would not last. One of the leaders of those who believed in the future of the internal-combustion engine was the Prince of Wales, and this drawing, when it was published in the *Illustrated London News* in 1904, marked a turning point. It was captioned 'The Old Power and the New. Familiarising the Prince of Wales's Horses with the Motor Car at Marlborough House. After a time the horses come boldly up to the car and rub their noses against it.'

131 Two into one won't go: When the rolling English drunkard made the rolling English road he did not make it wide enough for those new-fangled motor cars, as is plain from the photograph, taken near Dartmoor in 1913.

132 'Diabolo while the Motor gets Mended: the Pastime for Breakdowns'. That is how this picture was captioned when it appeared in the *Illustrated London News* of 1907. The caption-writer went on to explain that since its revival, the eighteenth-century game of diabolo had already over-run France and now promised to become equally popular in England; motorists on the Continent were carrying a set with them so that 'the time spent in inevitable repairs might be killed pleasantly'. The information was no doubt greeted with an appropriate snort in the bay windows of the clubs in St James's.

133   A Belsize car in 1910: Mrs H. G. D. Stuart, who lent me this charming photograph, writes: 'The car belonged to my mother, Mrs Gibbons. It is standing outside my mother's house, Cowley Manor, near Exeter. The chauffeur was Charles Brooks, originally taken on to look after a pony and trap and do some gardening. When in 1910 my mother decided to get a car she sent Charles to an uncle of mine at Hampton Wick, who taught him to drive and look after the car. When my mother asked Charles, on his return, what he thought of London, he replied: "It was all right, but everyone thought I was a furriner and I couldn't understand them".'

134   A good idea that went astray: This adver-tisement for the Electro-mobile, published in *Country Life* in April, 1907, puts forward the view that the electric car-riage is the cheapest and best motor for town use. Looking back with the advantages of hindsight, most of us wish that the electric carriage, and not the internal combustion engine, had won the con-test for the control of urban roads in those early days.

We Have Published Two Books About The Ideal Town Carriage.

One result of the recent Town Carriage Competition, in which the Electromobile obtained such a striking award, has been that many people, sceptical of the claims of the electric carriage as the cheapest and best motor for town use, have been led to investigate them.

We have printed the facts about the Electromobile, together with letters from users and full particulars about the Car itself, in a small book, which we shall be pleased to send to anyone writing for it.

We have also published a second book, which gives in a concise form the details of our garage system, by which for a fixed sum we guarantee to take all responsibility and cost attached to the upkeep of a car off your hand, and undertake to supply your private car, fully equipped and in perfect order, either day or night, whenever you may require it.

These two publications, which fully describe the Electromobile—the town carriage—may be obtained free on application to . . .

The Electromobile Co., 7, Curzon Street, Mayfair, London. W.

Electromobile The Town Carriage

135   'A Quiet Sunday in our Village': Mr Punch's comment on motoring on 6 June, 1906. The drawing explains the need for the activity in plate 129.

136 Mr Punch on road safety: The caption, in 1908, read: 'Now that motors are sweeping the children off the roads, the railway tracks remain their only available playground. At least you know where you are with a train'.

Undertones of war

From the beginning of the century, thoughtful people in Britain were aware that sooner or later there would be war with Germany. Few of them seem to have had any notion of the scale of the catastrophe that lay ahead. The three frivolous drawings on the following pages, published in *Punch* in 1909, 1910 and 1912, probably reflected fairly accurately the belief that when the war did come it would be all over in a matter of months. Looked on with hindsight, this misconception was no doubt the result of the long peace of nearly one hundred years, since 1815, during which Britain's wars had been either sideshows, or colonial campaigns in which only a handful of troops were employed. Few Edwardians were troubled by the prospect of Armageddon.

137   All over in a month or two? It is difficult to be certain whether this drawing, when it appeared in *Punch* of 16 June, 1909, was poking fun at the regular army's casual attitude to the coming struggle, or whether it merely reflected the ambivalence of *Punch*'s own readers. The ambivalence is plain enough: the coming struggle is already given the name of the Great War, by which it was to go down in history; yet the subaltern expects it to be over in the short space between August and November.

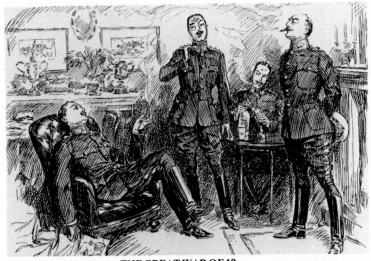

THE GREAT WAR OF 19—.

Major. "IT'S PRETTY CERTAIN WE SHALL HAVE TO FIGHT 'EM IN THE COURSE OF THE NEXT FEW YEARS."
Subaltern. "WELL, LET'S HOPE IT'LL COME BETWEEN THE POLO AND THE HUNTIN'."

139 (opposite)   The right date, but the wrong idea: The drawing, with its startling accuracy in predicting the date of the coming struggle, appeared in *Punch's Almanack* for 1912. Such total incomprehension of the nature of twentieth-century warfare may seem surprising to modern eyes, but it was little different from the asininity that sent English soldiers marching round the countryside in the winter of 1939–40 boasting that they would hang their mother's washing on the Siegfried Line.

138 'I knew no harm of Bonaparte, and plenty of the Squire': Wallis Mills's drawing of 12 January, 1910, is more a Chestertonian dig at the squirearchy than a comment on German military capacity; the little girls bob-curtsy dutifully even though the squire is looking the other way. Yet the picture must have reflected the general conviction that there was no real possibility of a successful German invasion —a conviction that remained as unshakeable thirty years later.

"WANTED, A MAN."

Canvasser. "HOW WOULD YOU LIKE THE VILLAGE OVERRUN WITH GERMANS? AND A GERMAN LIVING AT THE HALL?"
Villager. "WOT! THEM GERMANS TURN SQUIRE OUT? YOUNG MAN, YEW DON'T KNOW SQUIRE!"

Period—The War of 1914.

Furious M.F.H. (to invaders, who have made a dashing charge at supposed red-coated cavalry). "WHO THE DEUCE ARE YOU, AND WHAT ARE YOU PLAYING AT? D'YOU KNOW WHAT YOU'VE DONE, YOU CONFOUNDED SET OF TAILORS? YOU'VE—YOU'VE *HEADED THE FOX!*"

140, 141 & 142   The few who saw the danger: Most of the King's subjects, during the Golden Years, were happy to be lulled into a sense of false security. Only a few saw the danger, and did what they could by joining the Territorial Army and other voluntary reserves. These photographs of the oldest of all the voluntary forces, the Honourable Artillery Company, were taken during training at Bulford on Salisbury Plain in June, 1906. The equipment and training of these men had not greatly changed eight years later when the war began. It is doubtful whether even their individual devotion and foresight worked out to the national advantage when the test came. The HAC sent a battalion of infantry to Flanders in September 1914, almost all the men in the ranks being potential officers. They suffered fearful losses; in the battle of Hooges alone, in June 1915, casualties were 50 per cent.

The Daily Orders for 7 June, 1906, preserved with these photographs, are themselves of interest. Reveille for the Infantry Battalion HAC was at 4.0 am. In June, 1906, the rest of England was still fast asleep.

ЇDERS

BY

COLONEL THE EARL OF DENBIGH, C.V.O.,

Commanding Hon. Artillery Company.

Bulford 7ᵗ June 1906.

I Detail for tomorrow.— Friday

— H. A. Brigade —

Orderly Officer .... Lieut. D. Cooke
    Sergt .... Sergt. W. A. Hall
    Bombardier .... Bor. C. B. Gray

— Battalion —

Orderly Officer .... Lieut. L. Wright
    Sergt. .... Lce. Sgt. R. A. Robinson W. A. Stirling
    Corporal .... Cpl. L. M. Thompson
Post Orderly .... Pte. F. Bartlett

Medical Officer on duty :— Surg. Lt. J. F. Taylor

II Parades for tomorrow:—
The Horse Artillery will parade tomorrow as follows:—
"A" Battery will parade at such time as to reach Alton Barn South by 9.30 A.M.
"B"   11.30 A.M.
Haversacks & waterbottles to be worn. Lunch, feeds & cloaks to be carried.
All remaining ammunition to be carried.
Reveille at 5.0 A.M.
Stables - 5.30 .
Breakfast - 6.0 .
Boot & saddle - 7.0 .
The Infantry Battalion H.A.C. will take part in field operations tomorrow during
which it will be inspected by Major General Franklyn.
40 rounds blank ammunition per man will be carried.
Field service dress, one pouch, haversack & waterbottle will be worn.
Lunches to be taken.
Officers commanding Companies will ascertain from their colour sergeants that the
mens waterbottles are filled.
Reveille at 4.0 A.M.
Breakfast - 4.45 .
Parade - 5.45 .
Mard off - 6.15 .

III Maps :—
    All handkerchief maps must be returned to Orderly Room Tent by 6 P.M. tomorrow, Friday.
                                                    G. Stanley
                                            Captain & Adjutant H.A.C.

The closing moments

Everything that can be said about the closing moments of the Golden Years has been summed up by Philip Larkin in his poem *MCMXIV*, which he has generously allowed me to reproduce here:

Those long uneven lines
Standing as patiently
As if they were stretched outside
The Oval or Villa Park,
The crowns of hats, the sun
On moustached archaic faces
Grinning as if it were all
An August Bank Holiday lark;

And the shut shops, the bleached
Established names on the sunblinds,
The farthings and sovereigns,
And dark-clothed children at play
Called after kings and queens,
The tin advertisements
For cocoa and twist, and the pubs
Wide open all day;

And the countryside not caring:
The place-names all hazed over
With flowering grasses, and fields
Shadowing Domesday lines
Under wheat's restless silence;
The differently-dressed servants
With tiny rooms in huge houses,
The dust behind limousines;

Never such innocence,
Never before or since,
As changed itself to past
Without a word—the men
Leaving the gardens tidy,
The thousands of marriages
Lasting a little while longer:
Never such innocence again.